# Bernard Leach, Hamada
## & their Circle

from the
Wingfield Digby
Collection

# Bernard Leach, Hamada
## & their Circle

from the
Wingfield Digby
Collection

*Tony Birks & Cornelia Wingfield Digby*
*Introduction by Michael Webb*
*Photographs by Peter Kinnear*

Phaidon · Christie's
Oxford

Phaidon · Christie's Limited, Musterlin House,
Jordan Hill Road, Oxford OX2 8DP

First published in Great Britain in 1990

ISBN 0 7148 8075 2

A CIP catalogue record for this book
is available from the British Library

Designed and produced by
Alphabet & Image Ltd,
South Street, Sherborne,
Dorset DT9 3LU

Phototypesetting by LP&TS, Langport, Somerset
Printed and bound in Hong Kong by Regent Publishing Services Ltd

*Title page illustration*

**Bernard Leach : Lugged jar** Width 23 cm (9 in), height 25 cm (9¾ in)
Incised carp design wraps all around the pot between incised lines. Thick tenmoku glaze
inside, and outside to waist. Stoneware. On the side of the pot, near the foot, is a rare
incised BL mark with St Ives mark incised below.
*Date of acquisition unknown.*

# Contents

# *Introduction*

## by Michael Webb

The meeting of Bernard Leach and Shoji Hamada in 1919, over seventy years ago, started ripples which are still widening today and which may be considered one of the crucial events in twentieth-century ceramic history. The conversion to pottery of Bernard Leach, then living in Japan, began at a party in 1911 where each guest was invited to decorate a piece of raku which was immediately fired. His subsequent seeking out of the sixth Kenzan to train him, added a knowledge of traditional Japanese potting to that of conventional Western drawing (which he began to acquire at the age of sixteen under Henry Tonks at the Slade School of Art) and etching (which he learned under Frank Brangwyn at the London School of Art). By the time of his meeting with Hamada, Leach had already showed the versatility and imaginative diversity which was to be a hallmark of his output all his life. He had designed chairs, tables and bookcases, produced lithographs, etchings, drawings and paintings in both the Eastern and Western manner, and pottery ranging from raku lidded pots with bold simple floral designs to enamelled stoneware in Ko Kutani and the seventeenth-century German manner, as well as incised porcelain.

Shoji Hamada, aged twenty-four and eight years younger than Leach, was employed at the Ceramics Testing Institute in Kyoto, where in 1919 alone he made 10,000 test specimens of glaze. He sought out Leach, then living with Soetsu Yanagi, Leach's friend and mentor for life, to help him become a 'studio' potter. During the spring of that year, Leach decided to return to England and had saved, or been given, enough money for a pottery and for Hamada to come to assist him. The story of their meeting and the start of the pottery at St Ives has been movingly told in *Hamada, Potter* by Bernard Leach (Kodansha International, 1975). Together they built the first three-chamber climbing kiln seen in the West, and began firing in 1920.

The initial struggles were formidable — an absence of good local clay, little wood in an area long since depleted by tin-mining needs, problems with the kiln and a more than 20 per cent wastage. In 1923 (the year in which Michael Cardew joined the pottery at St Ives), Hamada returned to Japan. There he settled at Mashiko as a pottery hand in a district which supplied domestic ware to Tokyo some eighty miles south. After coming back to England to work and hold an exhibition at Paterson's Gallery, Bond Street, in 1929, he returned to start his own pottery. When Leach visited him at Mashiko in 1934 he was already well established. At a joint firing Leach was astonished at the arrival of some hundred or so visitors, mostly from Tokyo, to see the kiln opening.

By the time of the Dartington Conference, 1952, Hamada was world famous and, as the brief film of him at the wheel confirms, all who saw him throw found it an unforgettable experience. His pots at St Ives had been largely experimental and often combined traditional English and Japanese methods and materials. He destroyed all but the perfect after each firing and achieved some pieces of outstanding quality. On his return to Japan he seems to have found immediately that inimitable manner from which he never deviated and which makes a review of his work throughout his career unusually even. He was as remarkable a decorator as a thrower. Leach described both pots and potter as 'well-ballasted' and the powerful but sensitive brush and resist decoration exactly fit the forms. He worked in the rather coarse and unpliable local stoneware clay which he admitted took him twenty years to master.

In contrast to Leach, who struggled for recognition for much of his career, Hamada enjoyed success and security from his earliest days at Mashiko. He abandoned the habit of signing his work, begun at St Ives, and was never faced with the necessity of promoting himself as an individual artist/craftsman (in opposition to his beliefs), a dichotomy never quite solved by Leach. Hamada belonged to that tradition of individual Japanese potters stretching back to the sixteenth century and beyond. Leach had to create a 'tradition'.

Hamada's work and influence as a potter have been incalculable and it should not be forgotten that his belief in the meeting of East and West was no less powerful than that of Leach, despite its being more quietly stated. The two potters remained close friends all their lives with not infrequent visits by one or the other to Japan and England.

When George Wingfield Digby married Cornelia Keitler in 1935 he already possessed at least one piece of St Ives pottery, a small three-footed bowl, bought when an undergraduate at Cambridge in the late 1920s (see page 49). Shortly after their marriage they bought a jar by Katharine Pleydell-Bouverie and one (no longer in the Collection) by Norah Braden, neither of whom they had heard of. They did not start seriously 'collecting' pottery for another fifteen years. George Wingfield Digby had joined the textile department of the Victoria & Albert Museum in London in 1934. There was no vacancy in the ceramics department, an accident which left him free to collect pottery and porcelain without conflict of interest. The upheavals of the Second World War meant that it was not until 1950 that together they began nearly forty years of buying pottery and of growing friendships with Leach, Cardew and many other potters.

The potters in this book were chosen by George Wingfield Digby to illustrate the influence of Bernard Leach and Shoji Hamada at St Ives in the 1920s, together with one, Richard Batterham (working with Leach in the 1950s), whose pottery today demonstrates the continuation of that influence. Potters such as Lucie Rie, a close personal friend of Leach, and Janet Leach, his third wife, are not included as their styles are markedly different from that established in the early St Ives years.

Mr and Mrs Wingfield Digby collected pottery for love and use and their interests were unusually wide. The pieces illustrated, therefore, represent only a part of a larger collection of ceramics which ranges from Yixing teapots, Korean porcelain, Japanese nineteenth-century pottery, Chinese 'transitional' porcelain and Japanese porcelain from Imari to Kakiemon, as well as twentieth-century studio pottery.

On 29 April 1950 the Wingfield Digbys bought five pieces by Bernard Leach (total cost £16.11s [£16.55p]) at Heffers Bookshop in Cambridge, and then on 5 June at Charles Vyse's studio in London two large pots, a teapot and an open flower pot for £12.10s, £12.10s, £8 and £6 respectively, all by Shoji Hamada. They also bought eight pieces of Vyse's own pottery, including a tall vase at £12, as they felt uncomfortable at appearing to be interested only in Hamada (none of the Vyse pieces are now in the Collection). During this year they bought work by Constance Dunn, William Newland, Harry Davis and, in August, a glazed earthenware bowl from Lucie Rie, also ordering from her a morning tea set and a rectangular stoneware pen-tray to be in black and white at a cost of 30 shillings (£1.50p).

On 22 November 1950, at the Berkeley Galleries in London, they bought eight pieces from an exhibition of Michael Cardew's work for a total of £37.16s (£37.80p), with a top price of seven guineas (£7.35p).

Michael Cardew worked at St Ives from 1923 to 1926, as an apprentice, and set up his first pottery at Winchcombe in 1926, where he produced many of his finest pots. He believed passionately that pottery should be simple, useful and cheap. The Wingfield Digbys greatly admired him as man and potter, and found him an enchanting and stimulating friend. He came to have a consuming interest in the technical aspects of potting, and later regretted that he had found more comic than useful the talks by Tsurunosuke Matsubayashi, who worked at St Ives between 1922 and 1924, rebuilding the kiln and making a traditional Japanese kick-wheel for Katharine Pleydell-Bouverie.

On 8 October 1950 the Wingfield Digbys made their first visit to the Leach Pottery at St Ives, at a time when it was flourishing after the difficulties of the war. Bernard Leach's son, David, had returned from active service in 1945 and William Marshall joined in 1947. Bernard Leach had managed to continue potting throughout the war. The first illustrated mail-order catalogue was produced in 1946, and the reaction after austerity was a boon to traditional potters. The Wingfield Digbys made numerous purchases in October and November of that year.

In 1951, 12s.6d (62p) was paid for 'specimens' from Katharine Pleydell-Bouverie. At the age of twenty-nine she had persuaded Leach to take her for a year (1924) as what she described as a 'paying stooge'. Unlike Cardew, she paid close attention to Matsubayashi's talks, and when at the end of the year she set up her own pottery at Coleshill (the family house later destroyed by fire), she experimented with wood ash glazes, producing both bowls and glazes of exceptional beauty. In 1928 she was joined for eight years by Norah Braden, who had worked at St Ives from 1925 to 1928. Norah Braden was one of Leach's most gifted apprentice students, and he used one of her jars to illustrate the chapter 'Towards a Standard' in *A Potter's Book*, while he also illustrated a jar by Katharine Pleydell-Bouverie and used her extensive knowledge of glazes in Chapter 6. This knowledge she was still giving to any young potter who wrote to her up to her death in 1985 at Kilmington in Wiltshire, to where she moved her pottery in 1946.

In 1952 George Wingfield Digby published *The Work of the Modern Potter in England* (John Murray), which was, apart from T.G. Cooper's *The Modern Potter* (Tiranti, 1947), the first book to treat the subject adequately. Dora Billington's instruction at the London Central School made it possible for the author to write Chapter 3 'How Pottery is Made', and a notable feature is the attempt, largely the work of Cornelia Wingfield Digby, to illustrate pieces in an informal setting, as though being used, including flowers in several of the Leach Pottery examples. This emphasis on pots for use, rather than the museum display case, was a guiding principle of the whole Wingfield Digby Collection. The publication of this book resulted in many requests to George Wingfield Digby for introductions to catalogues and for reviews of exhibitions, and undoubtedly helped expand what was, and in some ways still is, a field of limited interest in the West.

In 1952 the first International Craft Conference of Potters and Weavers was held at Dartington Hall, Devon, for ten days. Largely initiated by Bernard Leach and sponsored by Leonard and Dorothy Elmhirst, it brought together leading craftsmen from all over the world. It was here that Cornelia first met Leach, arriving late at one of his talks ('Who are you? Sit down.'), and it was from there that they drove to St Ives to attend a kiln opening, the first of many. After Dartington, Leach, Hamada and Yanagi toured America for four months, lecturing on craft and the meeting of East and West. Leach then went to Japan, returning in 1954. He had intended to settle there permanently, but seems to have sensed that while lionized as a famous visitor he would be less welcome as a resident.

On his return to St Ives he bought back the Pottery from his son David, and he went through a most anxious period until Janet Darnell, an American whom Leach married in 1955, became manager in 1956 and instituted a regime essential to save the pottery from insolvency. It was from this period that Bernard Leach began, with the assistance of William Marshall, the making of 'exhibition' pots, which because of his increasing fame provided an additional income to that of the standard ware for which the pottery had long been well known. George and Cornelia Wingfield Digby very strongly rejected, however, the view stated recently that these pots represented Bernard Leach's 'finest achievement'.

From the earliest days at St Ives and throughout all the years the Wingfield Digbys visited the Pottery, the best pieces from each firing were set aside for exhibition and sale in Japan, where throughout his life Leach was far more famous than in the West, and where his work was always in demand.

The Wingfield Digbys eventually bought over 150 pots by Leach and thirty-five pieces by Hamada. The imbalance was caused inevitably by the scarcity and high prices of Hamada's work by the 1950s. They first met Hamada at the Dartington Conference and later Leach brought him to their London house, where they were delighted with his sense of humour. They recalled his interest in a pair of eighteenth-century Venetian chairs. Chairs, especially English country-made examples, had been of great fascination to him since his early days at St Ives, and he collected enough to give to craft museums in Japan as well as furnish his Mashiko house.

With Leach, Hamada was a staunch supporter of Soetsu Yanagi in his promotion of craftsmanship and its attendant philosophy, and whilst in England Leach expounded the values of Eastern thought and standards as an antidote to the sterility of mass production. Hamada, in a Japan rushing to industrialize, held up the values of traditional, often Western, craftsmanship.

In 1956 the Wingfield Digbys bought a flat in St Ives, in Barnaloft (a new building also containing studios) where Leach and others lived and Barbara Hepworth also worked. Previously they had stayed at the Porthminster Hotel, where Leach and George Wingfield Digby saw their first television set and remained motionless for two hours watching football and a show by Tommy Steele.

The Digbys found Leach the most delightful of friends, warm hearted, endlessly amusing and with a great passion for pottery and the graphic arts. He possessed the rare gift of revealing to others, by his words and gestures, hidden beauty in works of art, and taught them the Oriental way of considering every aspect of a pot which, though fundamental to an Eastern potter, was unknown in the West before his return from Japan. On walks he carried a balsawood drawing board with a pen and a bottle of Chinese ink in his pocket, drawing ceaselessly and often giving sketches to friends as he did when travelling in Japan. In his car he kept a spade and sack, and was not above purloining gravel from heaps of roadside materials to experiment with glazes.

*A Potter's Book*, first published in May 1940 (Faber & Faber), remains one of the outstanding books on any craft written this century, and contains most of Bernard Leach's views on pottery, especially in Chapter 1 'Towards a Standard'. In his talks with the Wingfield Digbys he would also stress the essential harmony of proportion in every pot — neck to body, width to height — and he would insist, for example, that the contrast between glazes of interior and exterior should mean that in a covered bowl the interior must be a surprise, that a fruit bowl should feel welcoming. He would emphasise that the form and especially the foot of a pot should give it 'spring'.

In the late 1950s (Leach was seventy in 1957) he was still capable of work beyond the physical scope of many younger men, but by now the larger 'exhibition' pots were thrown at his direction by William Marshall, leaving foot, rim and other details for Leach to complete. Marshall, from whom the Wingfield Digbys first purchased a piece in 1953, had joined the St Ives Pottery as the first of a series of local apprentices in 1938. He had an extraordinary gift for assimilating the style of visiting potters and was a superb thrower. He left the Pottery to start on his own in 1977.

On 5 January 1961 the Arts Council held the Bernard Leach 'Fifty Years a Potter' exhibition. To this Mr and Mrs Wingfield Digby loaned sixteen pieces, by far the most generous loan after those of the potter himself and of the Folk Craft Museum, Tokyo. Throughout the 1960s and early 1970s they continued to buy at St Ives, though in rather smaller numbers; in 1963, for five guineas (£5.25p), they acquired the drawing signed 'BL' of a bottle decorated with a spray of flowers (see page 38). In April 1977 they bought some ten pieces from Richard Batterham, who had worked at St Ives in 1957-8 and set up his pottery at Durweston, Dorset, in 1959. For the next ten years they bought many pieces from Batterham, who is widely regarded today as the best maker of domestic stoneware in Britain.

The influence on the practical and philosophical background to pottery in this century of both Bernard Leach and Shoji Hamada cannot be overstressed. Without them ceramics in the West and in Japan would be profoundly different. The influence of collectors such as George and Cornelia Wingfield Digby is less easy to assess, but in their practical support and knowledge of the Chinese, Japanese and Korean porcelain which they also collected, they brought to many potters that breadth of understanding and aesthetic sensitivity which is of very great benefit to all creative craftsmen. The examples of pottery in this book are a testimony equally to the men and women who made them and to the collectors who chose them.

# Bernard Leach

Bernard Leach was born in Hong Kong in January 1887 and remained in the Far East until he was 10. At the age of 16, he went to study drawing at the Slade under Professor Henry Tonks, and in 1909 he went to Japan as an etcher.

His first contact with pottery making was at a raku party near Tokyo in 1911, and from then until his death in 1979 pottery remained at the heart of a varied and creative life. Returning to England with Shoji Hamada, he set up the Leach Pottery in St Ives in Cornwall in 1920. Bernard Leach's career as a potter is very well documented, both in his own writing and in numerous books and catalogues on twentieth-century ceramics. He was passionate in his desire to introduce to Britain, at a time when craftsmanship was in decline, a feeling for harmony in pottery which he had learned in the Far East.

He returned many times to Japan and gained a reputation as a potter throughout the world which tended to overshadow his talents as a writer and a draughtsman. No one who knew him could remain unaffected by his enthusiasm as an artist and a communicator.

Bernard Leach was married three times and had three daughters and two sons - David and Michael - both of whom became potters. Two further generations now continue the family tradition.

Bernard Leach's most famous book *A Potter's Book* was published in 1940 - an inauspicious time, and an experience which he described as 'like hatching an egg in a thunderstorm'. A full list of Bernard Leach's publications is given in the bibliography on page 192.

Where there are several pots in an
illustration, the captions describe them in
the order left to right, or top to bottom.

**1 Large slipware dish** Diameter 33.5 cm (13¼ in), height 5.5 cm (2¼ in)
Japanese well-head design in black slip with BL below. Rim decorated with diagonal
strokes; all under galena glaze. Earthenware. Large BL signature in thick slip on unglazed
base, and St Ives seal. Made *c.*1925-30.
*Bought at the Berkeley Gallery, London, ex Edward Marsh collection, 1957.*

**2 Bowl** Diameter 29 cm (11½ in), height 12 cm (4¾ in)
Fritillary painted in cobalt and iron. Dark slip painted on rim and outside, with an ash
glaze overall. Stoneware. St Ives seal and BL painted on unglazed turned foot. Made *c.* 1950.
*Bought c.1960.*

14

**3 Squared-off jar** Width 18 cm (7 in), height 16 cm (6¼ in)
Beaten square after throwing. Decorated with combing on shoulders and combed Chinese
characters for man, woman, summer and winter on the sides. Ash glaze inside.
Stoneware. BL and St Ives seals on side near base.
*Bought at The Craft Centre, Hay Hill in 1950.*

FACING PAGE **4 Slipware charger** Diameter 46 cm (18 in), height 10 cm (4 in)
Painted design in iron slip of rampant beast with trailed trellis pattern on the rim.
Impressed rouletted design around rim. Banded and with slip-trailed wave pattern on
underside of rim. Galena glaze. Earthenware. Signed with decorative panel on glazed
base (above), 11 cm (4½ in) wide. Made in St Ives in 1929.

*Bought at the Berkeley Gallery, London in 1955 and exhibited in 'The Art of Bernard Leach'
exhibition at the Victoria and Albert Museum in 1977 and the St Ives exhibition in Tokyo in 1989.*

**5 Plate** Diameter 29 cm (11½ in), height 5.5 cm (2¼ in)
Thrown at the Leach Pottery and *decorated* by Bernard Leach with 'tree' design in brown
and grey. Brown rim. Stoneware.
*Bought at Primavera, London in 1950.*

**6 Bowl** Diameter 30.5 cm (12 in), height 11 cm (4½ in)
Design of three fritillaries on inside, the flower shape in paper-resist with sprayed
speckling around, and cobalt detailing on flower. Brush-painted leaves in iron. Ash glaze
inside, brown glaze outside. Stoneware. Signed BL under ash glaze on foot.
*Bought at Liberty's exhibition, London in 1956.*

**7 Lidded pot** Diameter 16 cm (6¼ in), height overall 18 cm (7 in)
Designed by Bernard Leach as a prototype for a jam jar to be produced at the St Ives
Pottery. Oatmeal glaze, decorated with bands and painted floral design, in iron oxide with
dots on the lid. Unglazed under edge of lid and rim. Stoneware. St Ives seal under glaze
near base and signed 'BL' in blue. Made in 1930s.
*Bought at Bendicks Chocolate Shop, Bond Street in 1959.*

**8 Jar** Width 26 cm (10¼ in), height 32.5 cm (12¾ in)
Incised banding and frond pattern through dark slip. Ash glaze, left bare near
base. Intense mottling from iron in clay. Stoneware. BL and St Ives and
'England' seals on side.
*Bought at the Leach Pottery, St Ives in 1959.*

**9 Large bowl** Diameter 23.5 cm (9¼ in), height 14 cm (5½ in)
Sgraffito leaf design, brushed over with iron detailing. Stilt marks on inside of bowl. Ash
glaze with iron mottling from the clay. Stoneware. BL and St Ives seals on unglazed
turned foot.
*Bought at Bendicks Chocolate Shop, Bond Street in 1959 and exhibited in
'The Art of Bernard Leach' exhibition at the Victoria and Albert Museum in 1977.*

**10 Vase** Width 10 cm (4 in), height 14 cm (5½ in)
The unusual quality of this special pot comes not from the shape or painted decoration,
but from the transmuting of the glaze from a glassy olive-green through lilac to matt
creamy white. It is a semi-oxidised chün glaze, using ash from thatchers' reed. The very
dark clay shows near the base. Stoneware. BL and St Ives seals are just clear of the glaze
near the base.
*Bought at the Crafts Centre of Great Britain in 1964.*

**11 Globular pot** Width 14.5 cm (5¾ in), height 14 cm (5½ in)
The glaze varies from waxy grey near the base to a dry straw colour near the top, with
globules where the glaze settled when the pot was held upside down in the glaze bucket.
The water-grass design, in iron with small flowers painted in black, extends all around the
pot, the fronds separated on the far side by an interesting rare 'BL' painted mark.
Stoneware. BL seal near base on side, St Ives seal inside unglazed foot. Made *c*.1927.
*Given to the Wingfield Digbys by the Very Rev. Eric Milner-White, Dean of York. Exhibited in the*
*'Fifty Years a Potter' exhibition at the Arts Council in 1961 and 'The Art of Bernard Leach'*
*exhibition at the Victoria and Albert Museum in 1977.*

**12 Small vase** Width 8.5 cm (3¼ in), height 10.5 cm (4¼ in)
Splashed runny olive-green glaze, with kaki spots.
Placed on kiln 'hot spot', the unglazed clay is
darkened by kiln ash. Stoneware. BL and St Ives seals
on side.
*A present from Bernard Leach, given in 1959.*

**13 Tea bowl** Diameter 15 cm (6 in), height 8 cm (3¼ in)
Sgraffito design enhanced with iron brushwork on
outside. Oatmeal glaze with iron spotting. Unglazed
lower third of outside darkened by kiln ash.
Stoneware. BL and St Ives seals on side.
*Bought in 1959.*

**14 Tile** 23 cm (9 in) square, 2 cm (¾ in) thick.
Painted iron design of bird feeding young with sgraffito detailing. Stoneware.
St Ives and illegible signature in lower corners. Eight St Ives seals impressed on back.
Made *c.* 1925.
*Bought in 1968.*

**15 Jar** Width 28 cm (11 in), height 33.5 cm (13¼ in)
Combed banding and incised scallop design on shoulder, largely infilled by thick
tenmoku glaze. The quality of this pot is enhanced by minor even blistering in the clay.
Stoneware. Large BL and St Ives seals on side under glaze near base, and 'England' seal
on base.
*Made in St Ives in 1958 and chosen from the kiln by George and Cornelia Wingfield Digby.*

27

**16 Jar** Width 18 cm (7 in), height 40 cm (15¾ in)
This unusual combination of a porcelain glaze on a stoneware clay came about when
Bernard Leach used this glaze on a pot previously discarded because the slip and
decoration had peeled and had been scraped off. Speckling from iron in the clay through
the glaze. Unturned base. Stoneware. Both the BL and St Ives seals on the side are
obscured by the thick glaze.
*Bought in 1972.*

**17 Vase** Width 16 cm (6¼ in), height 21 cm (8¼ in)
Grey-blue banding on waist, shoulder and neck. Brush design on two sides with pink
spots applied to design on top of the glaze. Stoneware. BL and St Ives seals under the
glaze near foot.
*Bought at the Bernard Leach exhibition at Liberty's, London in 1956.*

**18 Teapot** Diameter (bowl) 15 cm (6 in), height (less handle) 14 cm (5½ in)
Cobalt banding, bluish painting and pale spot design above the shoulder. Buff glaze
overall. Cane handle. Stoneware. St Ives seal obliterated by glaze. Made in 1951.
*Bought at the Leach Pottery, St Ives in 1957.*
*Exhibited in 'The Art of Bernard Leach' exhibition in 1977.*

**19 Bowl** Diameter 18 cm (7 in), height 10.5 cm (4¼ in)
Grey-green glaze, creamy white inside and on the rim where the glaze is thick. Stoneware.
Early script BL seal and St Ives seal inside foot. Made *c.* 1930.
*Bought in 1979 at Sotheby's, Belgravia, ex Dorothy and Leonard Elmhirst.*

**20 Bowl** Diameter 17 cm (6¾ in), width 6 cm (2½ in)
Flower design incised through iron painting to clay in centre. Jigger patterning on outside through iron banding. Glazed in white, brown spotting from kiln ash. Porcelain. BL and St Ives seals on opposite sides of foot.
*Bought in 1961 at the 'Fifty Years a Potter' exhibition at the Arts Council, 1961.*

**21 Plate** Diameter 18 cm (7 in), height 2.5 cm (1 in)
Flying goose or shag painted in iron in centre. Banded in iron and with fine incised line
near edge of rim and wavy incision on underside of rim. Some wood-ash speckling from
the kiln on inside of plate. Porcelain. BL and St Ives seals under glaze inside foot.
*Bought at Liberty's, London in 1956.*

**22 Flat dish** Diameter 31 cm (12¼ in), height 4.5 cm (1¾ in)
Tenmoku glaze inside and outside with rim wiped clean and Chinese character painted
on (in white slip, turning tenmoku to red). Glazed base. Stoneware. St Ives seal on
underside of rim.
*Bought in the 1960s.*

**23 Beaker vase** Width 10 cm (4 in), height 12.5 cm (5 in)
The glory of this pot is in the subtle contrast between the glaze and decoration, which is
on two sides, applied with a slip trailer on top of the olive-green glaze. Stoneware. BL and
St Ives seals on side. Made *c.* 1950.
*Date of acquisition unknown.*

**24 Elephant**
Length 6.5 cm (2½ in), height 4.5 cm
(1¾ in)
Tenmoku glaze. Solid clay with incised
patterning emphasised by the tenmoku
glaze. Stoneware. St Ives and unusual BL
seal stamped into the unglazed feet.
*Bought at the Leach Pottery, St Ives in 1950.*

**25 Lidded cigarette jar**
Width 10 cm (4 in), height overall 13 cm (5 in)
Thrown in one piece and cut, with flange
added later to lid. Sgraffito pattern on
both sides of the bowl under dark green-
blue glaze, also on lid. Modelled
elephant handle on lid. Stoneware.
St Ives and large BL seals on side, with
BL seal kept clear of glaze. Made *c.* 1950.
*Date of acquisition unknown.*

**26 Lidded box**
Diameter 10 cm (4 in), height 10 cm (4 in)
Domed top and bird knob. Two incised
bands on lid. Crazed celadon glaze inside
and outside (wiped clean from join
between lid and bowl). Stoneware.
Glazed turned foot with BL seal under
foot and St Ives seal on lower side.
*Bought at The Craft Centre, Hay Hill in 1954.*

**27 Watercolour of pot on rice paper** Painted in 1963.
*Bought at the Leach Pottery, St Ives in 1965, together with pot No. 28.*

**28 Vase** Width 11.5 cm (4½ in), height 19 cm (7½ in)
Floral spray design in cobalt with pink spots on both sides, painted over white glaze.
Stoneware. BL and St Ives seals near foot.
*Bought at the Leach Pottery, St Ives in 1965.*

**29 Vase** Maximum width 15 cm (6 in), height 28 cm (11 in)
Beaten oval and with free sgraffito design on the two flattened sides. Tenmoku glaze
reveals throwing lines. Stoneware. BL seal and St Ives seal near base on opposite sides.
*Bought at the Bernard Leach exhibition at Liberty's, London in 1956.*

**30 Vase** Width 12 cm (4¾ in), height 19 cm (7½ in)
Yingquing glaze over porcelain glaze, on fluted sides
near base. Porcelain. BL and St Ives seals.
Made *c.* 1968.
*Bought at the Leach Pottery, St Ives in 1968.*

**31 Vase** Width 11.5 cm (4½ in), height 11 cm (4¼ in)
Tenmoku glaze on fine clay. Turned foot. Stoneware. BL and
St Ives seals near base, obscured by glaze. Made *c.* 1955.
*Bought at the Bernard Leach exhibition at Liberty's,
London in 1956.*

**32 Small vase** Diameter 6.5 cm (2¾ in), height 8.5 cm (3½ in)
Fine clay indented with dimple on three sides. Glazed with kawai glaze. Stoneware. BL
and St Ives seals near unglazed base.
*Bought at The Craft Centre, Hay Hill in 1953.*

**33 Hexagonal box** Diameter 5.5 cm (2¼ in), height 4.5 cm (1¾ in)
Cut sides. Flower pattern incised on lid and filled
with cobalt. Porcelain. BL and St Ives seals on base.
Made *c.* 1971.
*Bought at the Leach Pottery, St Ives.*

**34 Circular box** Diameter 7.5 cm (3 in), height 5.5 cm (2¼ in)
Incised blue flower on lid. Transparent glaze over
cobalt. Porcelain. BL and St Ives seals on base. Made
in 1971.
*Bought at the Marjorie Parr Gallery, London.*

RIGHT **35 Hexagonal box** Diameter overall 6.5 cm (2½ in), height 4.5 cm (1¾ in)
Cut sides. Incised design on top and three sides, filled with white slip. Iron speckling from
clay. Stoneware. BL and St Ives seals on opposite sides near base.
*Bought at the 'Fifty Years a Potter' exhibition at the Victoria and Albert Museum, in 1961.*

**36 Powder box** Width 6.5 cm (2½ in), height 5 cm
(2 in)
White with incised decoration within blue bands, and
blue frog painted on the top. Pale celadon glaze.
Porcelain. BL incised and St Ives seal on glazed base.
*Made specially for Cornelia Wingfield Digby in 1960.*

**37 Plate** Diameter 14.5 cm (5¾ in), height 2 cm (¾ in)
The incised fish emphasised in cobalt. Thin iron
painting on underside combines with cobalt at rim.
Porcelain. BL script incised and filled with cobalt on
white glazed base; St Ives seal on underside of rim
and 'England'. Made *c.* 1960.
*Date of acquisition unknown.*

**38 Lidded box** Diameter 10 cm (4 in), height overall 8 cm (3¼ in)
Incised bands, emphasised by cobalt on lid and sides, with some cobalt painting over
repeating incised marks on the sides. Loop handle on lid shows signs of iron staining.
Transparent glaze. Porcelain. BL and St Ives seals near glazed foot. Made *c*. 1968.
*Bought at the Leach Pottery, St Ives in 1968.*

**39 Porcelain box** Width 3 cm (1¼ in), length 5.5 cm (2¼ in), height overall 4.5 cm (1¾ in)
Incised design of flying bird on one side, pecking bird on the other, with BL seal on one
end and St Ives seal on the other end. Scroll patterns on lid all incised and filled with
cobalt under pale-blue glaze. Made *c.* 1960.
*A gift to Cornelia Wingfield Digby from the potter.*

**40 Small tripod bowl** Diameter 10 cm (3¾ in), height 3.5 cm (1½ in)
Very finely incised around rim with repeating pattern. Glazed all over. Porcelain.
*Date of acquisition unknown.*

**41 Hexagonal box** Width 7 cm (2¾ in), height 4 cm (1½ in)
Kaki glaze on outside with Chinese character dripped
on to lid in tenmoku glaze. Celadon glaze inside, and
inside lid. Stoneware. BL script seal and St Ives seal
on turned base. Made in the 1960s.
*Date of acquisition unknown.*

**42 Bowl on tripod**
Width 10 cm (4 in), height overall 6 cm (2¼ in)
Chinese in form. Plain glaze all over. Stoneware.
*Bought at Primavera, Cambridge in 1929. The first pot
bought by George Wingfield Digby.*

**43 Ink and wash drawing of a lidded box**
Width 20 cm (8 in), height 15 cm (6 in) on hand-made paper
The work is clearly dated 1912, and was therefore painted in Japan when Bernard Leach
was 25 years old, only one year after he had been introduced to the art of pottery making
in Tokyo.
*Date of acquisition unknown.*

**44 Flat-sided bottle** Width 14 cm (5½ in), height 19.5 cm (7¾ in)
Pressmoulded in two pieces with added foot and neck. Tenmoku glaze breaking to rust on
corners. Willow decoration painted on both sides. High fired (1300°C) stoneware. BL and
St Ives seals inside unglazed foot.
*Bought at the Royal Horticultural Hall in 1957.*

**45 Vase** Width 12.5 cm (6 in), height 35 cm (13¾ in)
Leaf design incised on one side only. Hakeme white slip, with iron brush painting to
emphasise leaf design. Mottling through porcelain glaze from iron in clay. Stoneware. BL
and St Ives seals on side under glaze, and 'England' seal on turned foot.
*Bought at the Primavera exhibition, London in 1958, exhibited in the 'Fifty Years a Potter'*
*exhibition at the Arts Council in 1961, and used as a frontispiece to the catalogue.*

**46 Facetted vase** Width 9.5 cm (3¾ in), height 17.5 cm (6¾ in)
White clay covered with Yingquing glaze with some marks from kiln ash.
Porcelain. BL and St Ives seals near base. Made in 1968.
*Date of acquisition unknown.*

**47 Circular lidded box**
Diameter 8 cm (3 in), height overall 6 cm (2¼ in).
Thrown in two parts. Base turned and cut away to
make three feet. Three Chinese characters incised into
sides. Glazed with semi-matt Yingquing glaze, inside
and outside. Porcelain.
*Bought at the Leach Pottery, St Ives in 1961.*

**48 Stem cup**
Diameter 8.5 cm (3¼ in), height 6.5 cm (2½ in)
Thrown in two pieces. Transparent glaze. Porcelain.
BL seal inside raised stem, St Ives seal on outside of
stem.
*Date of acquisition unknown.*

**49 Celadon bowl** Diameter 14 cm (5½ in), height 5 cm (2 in)
Incised detailed decoration on exterior. Glazed under footring. Porcelain. BL and St Ives
seals.
*Date of acquisition unknown.*

**50 Vase for single flower**
Width 7 cm (2¾ in), height 9 cm (3½ in)
Thrown in dark clay. Glazed with
smokey-blue glaze with a few kiln ash
spots. Stoneware. BL, St Ives and
'England' seals on unglazed base. Made
late 1950s.
*Date of acquisition unknown.*

**51 Porcelain vase**
Width 10 cm (4 in), height 14.5 cm (5¾ in)
White glaze with slight brown speckling
from kiln ash. Unglazed turned base.
BL and St Ives seals on lower side.
*Bought at The Craft Centre, Hay Hill in
1955.*

**52 Vase for single flower**
Width 6.5 cm (2½ in), height 7.5 cm (3 in)
Tenmoku glaze with kaki pattern
dripped on. Stoneware. St Ives seal.
Made late 1950s.
*Date of acquisition unknown.*

57

**53 Bottle** Width 16 cm (6¼ in), height 17.5 cm (7 in)
Pattern of repeating scrolls incised through white slip and covered in white glaze. The
brown speckling comes from iron in the clay. Stoneware. BL and St Ives seals on unglazed
lower side, and 'England' stamped into unglazed turned base.
*Bought in 1973.*

**54 Bulbous vase** Width 10.5 cm (4 in), height 15 cm (6 in)
Six vertical grooves. Grey-green ash glaze. Stoneware. Incised script BL and early St Ives
seal on side near unglazed base. Made in the 1950s.
*Bought at Heffers Gallery, Cambridge in the early 1950s.*

**55 Teapot** Width (bowl) 11.5 cm (4½ in), height 12 cm (4¾ in)
White glaze over fine porcelain clay. Porcelain. BL and St Ives seals under glaze inside
foot. Made in 1963.
*Bought at Primavera, London in 1963. Exhibited, and illustrated in the catalogue of the Victoria
and Albert Museum's exhibition of 'The Art of Bernard Leach' in 1977.*

To Nellie
14.III.71
As hungry
For the sea
As any salmon
For the quiet pools
Upstream
BL
1964

**56 Ink and wash drawing, landscape with mountain stream**
Width 17 cm (6¾ in),
height 11 cm (4½ in)
The work is inscribed, initialled and dated 1964, and dedicated to Cornelia Wingfield Digby by Bernard Leach in 1971.
*A gift from the artist, 1971.*

**57 Vase** Width 12.5 cm (5 in), height 27 cm (10½ in)
Oatmeal glaze on upper part of pot with iron decoration. Stoneware. BL and St Ives seals
on unglazed side near deeply turned base.
*Bought at Heffers Gallery, Cambridge in 1950.*

**58 Vase** Width 18 cm (7 in), height 22 cm (8¾ in)
White slip overpainted in iron, leaving white bands, with fine stylised chrysanthemum patterns incised through the iron painting to reveal white slip below. Glazed in an oatmeal glaze inside and outside to just below the waist. Unglazed clay is kiln darkened to bright russet. Coarse turning on lower side. Stoneware. BL and St Ives seals.
*Exhibited at Liberty's, London in 1956 and South Africa in 1957. Bought at the Leach Pottery, St Ives in 1958.*

**59 Vase** Width 16.5 cm (6½ in), height 24 cm (9½ in)
Kaki glaze. A single blob of another glaze floats like the spot on Saturn on the beautiful
glaze, which so well complements the shape. Stoneware. Large BL and St Ives seals
impressed on side near unglazed base. Made *c.* 1950s.
*Date of acquisition unknown.*

**60 Ashtray** Diameter 11.5 cm (4½ in), height 5 cm (2 in)
Leach Pottery ashtray with oatmeal and kaki glaze, decorated by Bernard Leach. The two
thistles painted in iron oxide and cobalt. Stoneware. St Ives seal near base.
*Bought at the Leach Pottery, St Ives in 1955.*

**61 Beaker vase**
Width 8 cm (3¼ in), height 15 cm (6 in)
White porcelain, slightly speckled from
iron in clay. BL and St Ives seals on side
near base.
*Bought at Primavera, London in 1959.*

**62 Beaker vase**
Width 9 cm (3½ in), height 17 cm (6¾ in)
Dark-blue glaze. Stoneware. BL and St
Ives seals near base.
*Selected in St Ives in 1960 and bought at
Primavera, London in 1960.*

**63 Beaker vase**
Width 7 cm (2¾ in), height 12 cm (4¾ in)
Uneven dark rim and white glaze.
Porcelain. BL and St Ives seals near base.
*Bought at the Leach Pottery in 1967 during a
visit for the celebration of Bernard Leach's
eightieth birthday.*

**64 Lidded jar** Width 14 cm (5½ in), height overall 17 cm (6¾ in)
Tenmoku glaze outside, kaki glaze inside, and inside the lid. Stoneware. BL and St Ives
seals near unturned base.
*Bought at Primavera, London in 1963.*

**65 Globular pot** Width 12.5 cm (5 in), height 14 cm (5½ in)
Kaki glaze inside and outside with tenmoku brush marks and bands near rim. Stoneware.
BL and St Ives seals near unglazed turned foot.
*Date of acquisition unknown.*

**66 Bowl** Diameter 27 cm (10½ in), height 8.5 cm (3¼ in)
Combed wave pattern on outside with brown band above. White slip on *inside* of rim, and
making a spiral design in centre. Glazed overall with grey-blue glaze, showing iron
spotting from the clay. Stoneware. BL and St Ives seals on unglazed turned foot. Made in
1959.
*Bought at the Primavera exhibition, London in 1960.*

**67 Tea bowl** Diameter 13.5 cm (5¼ in), height 7.5 cm (3 in)
White hakeme slip on inside, glazed in grey overall with iron spotting from clay.
Stoneware. BL script painted inside unglazed foot in iron.
*Bought in 1968 at the kiln opening, St Ives, when Bernard Leach was given the Freedom of the Borough of St Ives.*

**68 Small pot** Width 9.5 cm (3¾ in), height 8.5 cm (3¼ in)
One fritillary scratched through hakeme slip with grey-blue ash glaze, speckled with iron from a dark clay. Stoneware. BL, St Ives and 'England' seals on unglazed side.
*Given to Cornelia Wingfield Digby by Bernard Leach in 1959.*

**69 Beaker vase** Width 10 cm (4 in), height 13 cm (5¼ in)
Oatmeal glaze over hakeme slip, with rock and iris design in iron. Stoneware. BL, St Ives and 'England' seals near unglazed base.
*Bought at the Leach Pottery, St Ives in 1955.*

**70 Vase** Diameter 12 cm (4¾ in), height 18 cm (7 in)
Ash glaze inside, dark-brown glaze outside and into
neck. One of a pair of pots made together; the other
pot was sent to Japan by Bernard Leach. Stoneware.
BL and St Ives seals partially under the glaze near the
foot. Described by George Wingfield Digby as 'an old
man's pot'.
*Bought at the Leach Pottery, St Ives in the late 1960s.*

**71 Miniature beaker**
Diameter 5.5 cm (2¼ in), height 6 cm (2½ in)
Incised line near rim. Glazed in palest blue-grey glaze.
Porcelain. BL seal under glaze on side and St Ives seal
on chamfer by base.
*Date of acquisition unknown.*

**72 Facetted bowl** Diameter 21.5 cm (8½ in), height 13 cm (5 in)
Cut-sided bowl with 12 facets on tall turned foot. Kaki glaze inside, viscous grey-blue
glaze outside. Stoneware. Rare incised BL and St Ives marks inside footring.
*Bought at the 'Fifty Years a Potter' exhibition at the Arts Council in 1961.*

**73 Bowl** Diameter 15.5 cm (6 in), height 6 cm (2¾ in)
Made in coarse orange clay and decorated with white slip splashes, blue bands and
flashes. Grey glaze, nearly transparent where thin. Stoneware. BL and St Ives seals on
unglazed turned base.
*A gift from the potter, c.1961.*

**74 Vase** Width 9.5 cm (3¾ in), height 12 cm (4¾ in)
Leach Pottery. Incised marking and combing under ash glaze. Stoneware. St Ives seal.
Made in the 1960s.
*Bought at the Leach Pottery, St Ives, c.1965.*

**75 Cut-sided vase**
Diameter 9.5 cm (3¾ in), height 11.5 cm (4½ in)
Eight-sided porcelain vase with matt off-white glaze.
BL and St Ives seals on one facet near base.
*This pot was kept in Bernard Leach's room in St Ives and bought from there by the Wingfield Digbys in 1965.*

**76 Honey pot** Diameter 10 cm (4 in), height 10 cm (4 in)
Thrown in one piece in porcelain; the lid was then cut away and the twisted strap handle added. There is a cut opening near the rim for the spoon. An off-white porcelain glaze covers both inside and outside, slightly darkened in the vertical flutes incised into the outside. Ash mottling from the kiln on one side.
*Bought c.1960.*

**77 Tea bowl** Diameter 14.5 cm (5¾ in), height 7.5 cm (3 in)
Coarse clay, splashed with white slip. Grey glaze. Chipped at rim. Stoneware. BL and St
Ives seals on unglazed foot.
*Bought at the Leach Pottery, St Ives in 1965.*

matt Tenmoku

glossey Tenmoku

£4

Transparent olive transparent

well fired Tenmoku

£6

nice spotted Tenmoku

good Tenmoku

£5

**78 Three sketches on paper** reproduced actual size.
Bernard Leach drew these lively sketches to assist George Wingfield Digby in making a
choice of pots unseen. The Wingfield Digbys bought the most expensive pot, which is
illustrated at the top of the facing page, No. 79.

TOP **79 Tea bowl** Diameter 12.5 cm (5 in), height 9 cm (3½ in)
Tenmoku glaze outside, olive-green crackled glaze inside. Stoneware. BL and St Ives seals
near unglazed turned foot.
*Bought at the Primavera exhibition, London in 1960.*

ABOVE **80 Oblong pen box** Width 14.5 cm (5¾ in), length 21.5 cm (8½ in), height 4 cm (1½ in)
Slab built in dark clay. Grey and then white glazes inside with combing through the white
glaze. Tenmoku outside. Stoneware. BL and St Ives seals on base.
*Bought at the Leach Pottery, St Ives in 1961.*

**81 One pint beer mug**
Width 11 cm (4¼ in), height 12.5 cm (5 in)
Tenmoku glaze outside, grey-green ash glaze inside
and on rim. Stoneware. 1951 seal opposite handle, BL
and St Ives seals filled with glaze, under handle.

**82, 83 Two half-pint beer mugs**
Width 7.5 cm (3 in), height 11.5 cm (4½ in)
Pale-olive ash glaze inside and on rim. Tenmoku on
outside. Stoneware. 1951 seals opposite handle, St
Ives seal under handle.

*Bernard Leach designed these mugs for the 'Britain Can Make It' exhibition
in 1951. All were bought at the Leach Pottery, St Ives in that year.*

**84 Lidded stewpot**
Width overall 20 cm (8 in), height 14 cm (5½ in)
Strap lugs and incised wave pattern on both sides through thick tenmoku glaze.
Kaki glaze inside. An interesting detail is that Bernard Leach pressed in the
sides of the pot, below the lugs, to facilitate handling. Stoneware. BL and St
Ives seals on side below lug.
*Bought in 1983.*

**85 Tea bowl** Diameter 9.5 cm (3¾ in), height 9 cm (3½ in) Rich chestnut-brown glaze inside and outside, with two ears of corn incised through brown to a lighter glaze below. Unglazed turned base. Stoneware. BL script incised into the side together with St Ives seal. *Bought at Heffers Gallery, Cambridge in 1950.*

· **86 Tea bowl** Diameter 10 cm (4 in), height 7.5 cm (3 in) Runny kaki glaze. Stoneware. St Ives seal under glaze near unglazed foot. *Date of acquisition unknown.*

**87 Bowl** Diameter 20 cm (8 in), height 7 cm (2¾ in)
Clear glaze inside with small flower painted in iron and flecked with ash from the kiln.
Outside, a repeating pattern and bands are scratched through iron slip, which turns the
porcelain glaze overlying it an interesting reddish brown. Porcelain. BL and St Ives seals
inside unglazed foot, 'England' on outside of foot.
*Bought at the Leach Pottery, St Ives in 1961.*

**88 Coffee pot** Width 11 cm (4½ in), height 16.5 cm (6½ in)
Incised tooled decoration under tenmoku glaze. Pulled handle has unusual lower fixing.
Spout applied to opening cut into the side below recess for lid. Stoneware. Large BL seal
near base.
*Bought at the Primavera exhibition, London in 1960.*

TOP **89 Covered bowl** Diameter 10 cm (4 in), height overall 7 cm (2¾ in)
Thrown in one piece, cut, and flange added to lower part. Incised pattern on lid. Celadon
glaze. Stoneware. BL and St Ives seals on glazed base.
*Bought at the Leach Pottery, St Ives.*

**90 Small dish** Diameter 12 cm (4¾ in), height 2 cm (¾ in)
One of a set of five small food dishes for Japan. Design combed through white
slip, under transparent glaze. Tenmoku glaze outside. Unglazed base. Stoneware. BL and
St Ives seals on opposite sides. Made in the 1960s.
*Date of acquisition unknown.*

**91 Tea bowl** Diameter 15 cm (6 in), height 6.5 cm (2½ in)
Kaki and tenmoku glazes on outside covering an incised wave pattern decoration, with
crackled rice-husk glaze inside and running over the rim. Glazed inside footring.
Stoneware. Unusual BL seal under the glaze near the foot.
*Made in Japan at Mashiko in 1955 for the Tokyo exhibition of tea bowls and brought back by
Bernard Leach for the Wingfield Digbys after the exhibition.*

**92 Vase** Diameter 10 cm (4 in), height 15 cm (6 in)
Toothed pattern incised diagonally. Runny ash glaze inside and outside. Dark clay.
Stoneware. BL, St Ives and 'England' seals on side.
*Bought at Primavera, London in 1963.*

**93 Jug** Height 14 cm (5½ in)
Applied thumbed knob decoration and repeating thumbnail marking on pulled handle.
Tenmoku glaze. Stoneware. BL and St Ives and 'England' seals at base of handle.
*Bought at the Penwith Gallery exhibition, St Ives in 1960.*

**94-97 Mead jug with three stem cups**
Jug: width 13.5 cm (5¼ in), height 19 cm (7½ in)
Cups: width 8 cm (3¼ in), height 7 cm (2¾ in)
Celadon glaze. Stoneware. St Ives and 'England' seals on sides.
*Bought at the Leach Pottery, St Ives in 1958.*

**99 Small pot** Width 9 cm (3½ in), height 8.5 cm (3¼ in)
Celadon glaze with incised band near rim. Fritillary painted in iron. Stoneware. Unglazed
foot, with St Ives seal and BL script under glaze on side. Made *c.* 1935.
*Bought at Sotheby's, Belgravia in 1979.*

FACING PAGE **98 Jug** Width 14.5 cm (5¾ in), height 24.5 cm (9¾ in)
Tenmoku glaze over fine clay. Designed by Bernard Leach for the 1951 Festival of Britain,
derived from medieval shape. Unturned base. Stoneware. St Ives seal under handle.
*Bought at the Leach Pottery, St Ives in 1951.*

# *Shoji Hamada*

Shoji Hamada was born in Tokyo in 1894, and, influenced by many notable potters, devoted his life to pottery from the age of 16. He first met Bernard Leach in 1918, and by 1920 had travelled with him to England to found the Leach Pottery in St Ives.

Michael Cardew has written: 'The landing of Bernard Leach and Shoji Hamada on the island of Britain in 1920 was for craftsmen potters the most significant event of the twentieth century.' Although he only stayed three years, in that time was forged the creative and personal bond which lasted throughout the lives of the two potters, and indeed outlives them both.

He returned to Japan in 1923, and in 1925 held the first of many annual one-man shows in Tokyo. In 1930 he established his home and pottery in Mashiko, 100 miles north of Tokyo, where he and his family developed a perfect pattern of work and life. Mashiko became a place of pilgrimage for potters from many countries, whilst Hamada himself frequently visited Britain and toured the world, sometimes in company with Bernard Leach.

Hamada rarely signed or stamped his pots, believing that the identity of the artist should reveal itself in the work. The characteristic brushwork on his pots, based on an image from a ricefield devastated by a downpour, and the glazes of which he was the acknowledged master, are a testimony to this view, and Hamada is regarded by many as the greatest potter of the twentieth century.

He was the recipient of numerous cultural honours in Japan and in America and in Britain; he died at Mashiko in 1978.

**100 Nine-sided jar** Width 23 cm (9 in), height 22.5 cm (8¾ in)
Ash glaze with three wax-resist designs on sides and three flecks on shoulders, covered in
kaki glaze. Stoneware.
*Bought in 1956.*

**101 Vase** Width 20 cm (8 in), height 35 cm (14 in)
Olive-green glaze, hakeme slip, overpainted with tree design in iron on both sides. Glazed
foot. Stoneware. Made in the 1930s.
*Bought from Charles Vyse in 1950.*

**102 Vase** Width 20 cm (8 in), height 35 cm (14 in)
Greenish transparent glaze with wax-resist design on both sides, overpainted in iron slip.
Glazed foot. Stoneware. Made in the 1930s.
*Bought from Charles Vyse in 1950.*

**103 Wide-topped vase** Width 16 cm (6¼ in), height 13.5 cm (5¼ in)
White slip over dark clay. Floral pattern overpainted in iron and cobalt. Transparent glaze
outside. Olive-green glaze inside. Stoneware. Made in the Ryukyu Islands.
*Bought from Charles Vyse in 1950.*

**104 Teapot** Width (bowl) 14.5 cm (5¾ in), height overall 17 cm (6¾ in)
Tenmoku glaze over a twelve-sided form. Facetted strap handle. Lid unglazed inside.
Stoneware. Used by George Wingfield Digby in his office at the Victoria and Albert
Museum.
*Bought from Charles Vyse in 1950.*

**105 Facetted bowl** Diameter 22 cm (8¾ in), height 12.5 cm (5 in)
Cream coloured crazed glaze. Stoneware.
*Bought in the 1950s.*

**106 Incense box** Width 5 cm (2 in), height 5 cm (2 in)
Made in red clay, thrown, beaten and cut. Grey glaze
with flower design in iron drops on top. Slight
crawling. Stoneware.
*Bought in the 1960s.*

**107 Yunomi** Width 9 cm (3½ in), height 9 cm (3 in)
Combed pattern of alternating bars, glaze varies from
pale lilac to dark green where thin. Glazed inside
foot. Stoneware.
*Bought in the 1960s.*

**108 Sake bottle** Width 10 cm (4 in), height overall 23.5 cm (9¼ in)
Four-sided, slab built. Grey ash glaze with thick brilliant white slip on sides (and base).
Iron oxide painted designs on each side. Slight crawling. Stoneware. Made in Mashiko.
*Sent as a gift by the potter in 1962.*

**109 Bowl** Diameter 22 cm (8½ in), height 9 cm (3½ in)
Coloured slip on rim shows blue through grey glaze. Rim painted with iron. Motifs
painted inside with iron pigments. Glaze crawls near foot on outside. Stoneware. Made in
Mashiko.
*Bought at the Hamada exhibition at The Craft Centre, Hay Hill in 1958.*

**110 Square dish** Width 19.5 cm (7¾ in), height 4 cm (1¼ in)
Pressmoulded in light-grey clay, quartered in tenmoku with brush design and glazed on
rim with rice-husk glaze. Stoneware. Made in Mashiko.
*Bought at the Crafts Centre of Great Britain in 1963.*

**111 Vase** Width 17 cm (6¾ in), height 31 cm (12¼ in)
Kaki glaze inside. White rice-husk glaze (nuka) over tenmoku outside, greeny-brown
where the glazes overlap. Three finger-wipe designs. Stoneware. Made in Mashiko.
*Bought at the Crafts Centre of Great Britain in 1963.*

**112 Yunomi**
Width 7.5 cm (3 in), height 9 cm (3½ in)
Light slip outside on top half, covered
with grey glaze which starts to crawl on
the lower half. Iron painted on rim and
iron design on both sides. Glazed foot.
Stoneware. Made in Mashiko.
*Bought at the Hamada exhibition at The
Craft Centre, Hay Hill in 1958.*

**113 Yunomi**
Diameter 9 cm (3½ in), height 9 cm (3½ in)
Tenmoku glaze with finger marking.
Green-grey glaze inside. Stoneware.
Made in Mashiko.
*Bought in the 1960s.*

**114 Yunomi**
Diameter 8 cm (3¼ in), height 8.5 cm (3½ in)
Undulating combed decoration through
kaki slip, with transparent glaze on
outside, and white rice-husk glaze inside,
running over rim. Made with fine clay.
Stoneware.
*Bought in the 1960s.*

**115 Bowl** Diameter 26.5 cm (10½ in), height 5 cm (2 in)
Tenmoku glaze with looped ladle-poured design in kaki. Wide footring. Stoneware.
*Bought at the Hamada exhibition at The Craft Centre, Hay Hill in 1958.*

**116 Yunomi** Width 8.5 cm (3¼ in), height 9 cm (3½ in)
Green ash glaze, breaking on ridge on side. Greenish-
black and brown brush marks. Unglazed turned foot.
Stoneware. Made in Mashiko.
*Bought at the Hamada exhibition at The Craft Centre, Hay
Hill in 1958.*

**117 Yunomi** Width 8.5 cm (3¼ in), height 9 cm (3½ in)
Tenmoku glaze outside, wiped off the rim, green-grey
glaze inside running over rim. Glazed footring.
Stoneware.
*Bought in the 1960s.*

**118 Facetted vase** Width 12.5 cm (5 in), height 25 cm (9¾ in)
Thinly thrown. Olive-green glaze over a light clay. Base shows shell marks as the pot was
fired standing on shells. Stoneware.
*Bought in Japan in the 1960s.*

**119 Tea bowl** Diameter 12.5 cm (5 in), height 9.5 cm (3¾ in)
Rice-husk glaze over dark slip. Glazed inside footring. Iron glaze markings dripped on.
Stoneware.
*Bought in the 1970s.*

**120 Brush pot** Width 9 cm (3½ in), height 12.5 cm (5 in)
Kaki glaze inside and outside, with rice-husk glaze over outside and with iron glaze
patterning. Unglazed base. Stoneware.
*Bought in the late 1960s.*

**121 Tea bowl** Diameter 12.5 cm (5 in), height 8.5 cm (3½ in)
Tenmoku glaze with iron markings, glazed base. Stoneware.
*Brought back for the Wingfield Digbys from Japan by Bernard Leach in the 1960s.*

**122 Brush pot** Width 16 cm (6¼ in), height 14 cm (5½ in)
Impressed design repeated around outside. Thin tenmoku glaze on inside and, as two
bands, on outside. Rice-husk glaze on outside changing colour where glazes overlap.
Stoneware. Made in Mashiko.
*Bought at the Crafts Centre of Great Britain in 1963.*

# Michael Cardew

Michael Cardew was born in 1901, and was first drawn to pottery as a child in Devon, where the Fishley pottery at Fremington was still maintaining the English slipware tradition. Coming down from Oxford in 1923, he joined the Leach Pottery in St Ives in the summer of that year, just before Hamada returned to Japan, and stayed there for three years. In 1926 he took over the Winchcombe Pottery in Gloucestershire, making mainly traditional slipware until 1939.

In 1939 he moved to Wenford Bridge in Cornwall, and the Wenford Bridge Pottery, where he produced earthenware and stoneware, remained his base in Britain for the rest of his life. However, from 1942 to 1948, and from 1951 to 1965 he worked in Africa at Vumë in Ghana and Abuja in Northern Nigeria respectively, introducing wheel-made pottery and stoneware to African pupils, and at the same time developing and extending the range of his own work.

A fine musician, and a man of wide-ranging interests and talents, he demonstrated pottery-making and lectured around the world. His book *Pioneer Pottery* was published in 1969. He died in Cornwall in 1983, and an unfinished autobiography, *A Pioneer Potter*, was published in 1988.

**123 Small jug** Width 10.5 cm (4¼ in), height 10.5 cm (4¼ in)
A rich toffee-brown with darker undulating design, combed through white slip. Galena glazed earthenware. Winchcombe Pottery seal on unglazed unturned base. Made in the late 1920s to early 1930s.
*Date of acquisition unknown.*


**124 Small bowl** Diameter 12 cm (4¾ in), height 5 cm (2 in)
Toffee-brown glaze with deeper brown transverse wave design combed through white slip. Winchcombe Pottery seal on unglazed unturned base. Made in the late 1920s to early 1930s.
*Date of acquisition unknown.*

**125 Lidded tobacco jar** Width 14 cm (5½ in), height overall 17 cm (6¾ in)
The lid and upper part of the bowl covered with white slip with incised banding and
scroll design painted in iron oxide under a warm amber-yellow galena glaze.
Earthenware. Winchcombe Pottery seal on unglazed base with chamfer turning.
Made *c.* 1930.

*Bought in an antique shop in 1954.*

**126 Low bowl with wide rim** Diameter 18 cm (7 in), height 5 cm (2 in)
Incised quatrefoil design through white slip, galena glazed earthenware. Winchcombe
Pottery mark on base of turned unglazed foot, *c.* 1929. This pot shows signs of coal-
blowing from the early firings at Winchcombe.
*Date of acquisition unknown.*

**127 Bowl** Diameter 19 cm (7½ in), height 7.5 cm (3 in)
Two freely drawn fish on both interior and exterior in ochre and light-rust pigment under
a slightly speckled light-oatmeal glaze. Brown bands strongly defined at rim, below
exterior pattern and inside glazed foot. Wenford Bridge and MC seals stamped on glazed
base of turned foot.
*Bought at the Berkeley Gallery, London in 1950.*

**128 Vase** Width 16.5 cm (6½ in), height 22.5 cm (8¾ in)
Vumë liana-style decoration. Reddish-brown coloration from iron oxide. Stoneware.
Wenford Bridge and MC seals on unturned base, showing reddish-buff clay. Made at
Wenford Bridge in 1950.
*Bought at the Berkeley Gallery, London in 1950.*

**129 Small lidded jar** Width 10 cm (4 in), height overall 12 cm (4¾ in)
Applied and tooled rib decoration covered first with light slip and then with a clay-rich
glaze of dark brown breaking to amber. Stoneware. MC and Wenford Bridge seals on
turned foot under splash of glaze, showing red-brown clay.
*Reserved from Wenford Bridge exhibition in Camelford in October 1982.*

**130 Bowl** Diameter 26 cm (10¼ in), height 11.5 cm (4½ in)
Full rounded shape with a bird filling the interior together with palm fronds, brushed in
iron, fired to grey, and breaking to rust under a light-grey glaze. Banded on the rim, on
outside and within the turned footring. Stoneware. Wenford Bridge and MC seals on foot.
*Reserved in July 1950 at Wenford Bridge and bought at the Berkeley Gallery, London in November
of that year.*

**131 Jug** Diameter 15 cm (6 in), height 21 cm (8¼ in)
Outside, a russet-brown glaze with metallic flecking;
inside, cool grey-green. Stoneware. Embossed '1951'
— one of the several jugs prepared for the 'Britain
Can Make It' exhibition on the South Bank, London
in 1951. Wenford Bridge and MC seals on turned base.
*Bought at Heffers Gallery, Cambridge in 1951.*

**132 Jug** Diameter 15 cm (6 in), height 21 cm (8¼ in)
Fine white glaze. Incised bands near base. Stoneware.
Wenford Bridge and MC seals on turned and glazed
base. Embossed '1951'.
*Bought at Wenford Bridge in 1951.*

**133 Vase** Width 20 cm (7¾ in), height 24 cm (9½ in)
Globular form with pronounced neck. Semi-matt viscous glaze, tooled with Vumë pattern
and rilled. Stoneware. Wenford Bridge and MC seals on unturned base.
*This pot, with others, was reserved on a visit to Wenford Bridge in July 1950 and bought at the
Berkeley Gallery exhibition in November of that year.*

**135, 136 Pair of hanging cups** Width 10 cm (4 in) and 11 cm (4¼ in), height (both) 16 cm (6¼ in)
Painted Vumë lily pattern, purple clay. Stoneware. Vumë and MC seals on unglazed bases.
*Bought at the Sheila Harrison Gallery, London in August 1988; these pots were the last pieces
added to the Wingfield Digby Collection before George Wingfield Digby's death.*

LEFT **134 Soya sprinkler bottle** Width 9 cm (3½ in), height 11 cm (4¼ in)
The bottle has a screw top. Grey glaze with iron rust outbreaks on fluting. Reddish-brown
clay. Thrown spout. With Michael Cardew's customary attention to detail, he made only a
small hole in the body between pot and spout to prevent the sauce from rushing out.
Stoneware. Abuja and MC seals on side of unglazed foot.
*Bought at the Berkeley Gallery, London, Michael Cardew's Abuja Exhibition, 1958.*

**137 Lidded casserole** Diameter 23 cm (9 in), height overall 14 cm (5½ in)
Purple-brown clay, with pale streaks on the green glaze inside the casserole. Stoneware.
Abuja seal on the unglazed base. Made in Abuja, Northern Nigeria in the 1950s.
*Bought at the Berkeley Gallery, London in 1959.*

ABOVE AND FACING **138 Double bowl** Diameter 20.5 cm (8 in), height overall 11.5 cm (4½ in)
The lid serves as a subsidiary bowl. Purple-brown clay with Vumë lily pattern in dark
ferruginous brown, flashing russet-red under the glaze, also on the inside of the larger
bowl. Stoneware. Vumë and MC seals on the base of the turned and glazed foot, also on
top of the lid (i.e. the foot of the secondary bowl). Made in Vumë, Upper Volta.
*Brought back from Africa by Michael Cardew in 1952-3 as a gift, and used on his journey for his meals.*

**139 Bowl** Diameter 20 cm (8 in), height 7.5 cm (3 in)
On exterior two incised lines filled with white slip, with similar lines near centre of
interior. White glaze pattern trailed on to interior, over dark-brown glaze. Stoneware. This
Wenford Bridge bowl was almost certainly decorated by Michael Cardew.
*It was bought from Wenford Bridge in the late 1970s for use in the Wingfield Digbys' St Ives flat.*

**140 Bowl** Diameter 24 cm (9½ in), height 11 cm (4½ in)
Interior decorated with blue roundel and cobalt and iron brushwork. Grey-blue wave
pattern on exterior between iron bands. Grey glaze over slip. Glazed inside turned foot.
Stoneware. Wenford Bridge and MC seals near foot. Made in 1979.
*Bought at Camelford North Cornwall Gallery in 1979.*

# Katharine Pleydell-Bouverie

Katharine Pleydell-Bouverie was born in 1895, and, influenced by the Omega Workshop pots of Roger Fry, first studied at the Central School of Arts and Crafts. She joined Bernard Leach in St Ives in 1924, after meeting him in London the previous year. As with many potters who entered the Bernard Leach circle, this was to be the turning point in her life, and in the year she spent in St Ives as 'odd-job boy' she learnt a great deal from all at the Pottery, including Hamada and the kiln builder Matsubayashi.

She founded the Cole Pottery at the mill cottage on her family's estate in Berkshire, in 1925, and up to the outbreak of the Second World War she worked there with Ada Mason and then Norah Braden on a celebrated series of stoneware glaze tests. George Wingfield Digby wrote:

> 'Using a wide range of vegetable ashes, she produced some of the loveliest glaze effects known to stoneware pottery, with their soft luminous depths and matt surfaces in varied tones. . .
> . . These ash glazes worked out with great resourcefulness, have given to modern pottery in England a range of possibilities probably unparalleled elsewhere.'

After 1946 and up to her death in 1985, she continued her potting at Kilmington Manor in Wiltshire, and a correspondence with Bernard Leach in St Ives which was humorous, down-to-earth, but often profound. She was always self-deprecating about her own work, which she sold at absurdly low prices, and immensely generous and helpful to others. 'Beano', as she was always known, was one of the most influential and popular members of the circle of Bernard Leach.

**141 Vase** Width 19.5 cm (7¾ in), height 27.5 cm (10¾ in)
Incised patterning, obscured by banding in oxide, under semi-matt glaze. Glazed over
very dark clay. Stoneware. Made in the Cole Pottery at Coleshill.
*Bought in 1936 at Primavera, Cambridge — the first pot bought together by the Wingfield Digbys,
for use as a flower vase.*

**142 Small bottle** Width 7.5 cm (3 in), height 16 cm (6¼ in)
Thick glaze runny on one side, dry on the other.
Stoneware. KPB and Cole seals on unturned base.
Kept by Katharine Pleydell-Bouverie at Kilmington
with date finely painted in green paint on the base.
*Bought at Kilmington Manor sale in 1985.*

**143 Small bottle** Width 6.5 cm (2½ in), height 12.5 cm (5 in)
Thinly glazed in dark brown and grey-blue.
Stoneware. KPB and Cole Pottery seals on unturned
base. Made about 1927 and kept at Kilmington Manor
by the potter.
*Bought at Kilmington Manor sale in 1985.*

**144 Open bowl** Diameter 18 cm (7 in), height 7.5 cm (3 in)
Waxy white glaze on outside and over spiral incised pattern on inside. Stoneware. Made
early 1970s.
*Date of acquisition unknown.*

**145 Fluted bowl** Diameter 11 cm (4¼ in), height 7.5 cm (3 in)
Spiral fluting gives foliated shape to the flattened rim. Stoneware. KPB seal covered by
ash glaze.
*Bought at Primavera, London in 1956.*

**146 Glaze test** Diameter 5.5 cm (2¼ in), height 6 cm (2½ in)
Ash glaze, ground off the base. Glaze number
inscribed under foot. Stoneware.
*Date of acquisition unknown.*

**147 Pot** Diameter 8 cm (3¼ in), height 7 cm (2¾ in)
Stoneware. KPB seal on side near unglazed turned
base.
*Bought at Primavera, London in 1956.*

145

**148 Small fluted pot** Width 8.5 cm (3¼ in), height 6 cm (2½ in)
Glazed thickly in grey-blue over porcelain clay. The authenticity of this pot, asserted by
Tony Birks, is not confirmed by Cornelia Wingfield Digby. Turned foot. Porcelain.
KPB seal may be hidden under the glaze.
*Date of acquisition unknown.*

**149 Glaze test** Diameter 5.5 cm (2¼ in), height 5.5 cm (2¼ in)
Incised spiral pattern under turquoise ash glaze.
Stoneware.
*A gift from the potter c. 1960.*

**150 Bottle** Width 9 cm (3½ in), height 10 cm (4 in)
Ash glaze over red clay. Stoneware. KPB seal.
Probably made in the 1930s.
*Date of acquisition unknown.*

**151 Fluted glaze test**
Width 6.5 cm (2½ in), height 5.5 cm (2¼ in). Dark
glaze on red clay. Stoneware. KPB seal on the side.
*Bought at Heffers Gallery, Cambridge in 1951.*

**152 Glaze test in the shape of an oil jar**
Width 5 cm (2 in), height 5.5 cm (2¼ in). Glaze
number inscribed under foot. Stoneware.
*Date of acquisition unknown.*

147

**153 Small bowl** Diameter 9 cm (5½ in), height 4 cm (1¾ in)
The foliated pattern on the wide flat rim is created by the repeated ribbing on the outside.
Turned base. Stoneware.
*Date of acquisition unknown.*

**154 Cache-pot** Diameter 20 cm (8 in), height 18 cm (7 in)
Incised bands and wave pattern on outside. Glazed overall in poplar ash glaze.
Stoneware. Made *c.* 1950.
*Date of acquisition unknown.*

**155 Bowl** Diameter 9 cm (3½ in), height 11.5 cm (4½ in)
Thorn ash glaze overall, emphasising throwing lines. Stoneware. KPB seal near unglazed
turned foot.
*Bought at Primavera, London in 1956.*

**156 Bowl** Diameter 14 cm (5½ in), height 8 cm (3¼ in)
Turquoise glaze, heavily crazed inside and outside, over narrow vertical fluting on
outside. Stoneware. KPB seal on unglazed area near turned base. Made *c.* 1970.
*Date of acquisition unknown.*

# Norah Braden

Norah Braden was born in 1901 and came to the Leach Pottery in 1924 from the Royal College of Art on the recommendation of Sir William Rothenstein.

Both her work and her critical abilities were much appreciated by Bernard Leach, who described her as his most gifted pupil, and by Michael Cardew, who was her contemporary at St Ives. A highly self-critical potter, Norah Braden destroyed much work which did not satisfy her, and her output at St Ives was small. In 1928 she joined Katharine Pleydell-Bouverie at the pottery in Coleshill which the latter had started in 1925. The two potters were given an exhibition by Muriel Rose at her Little Gallery in London in 1929 and by Patersons in Bond Street in 1930. It was unusual for potters to receive critical attention from the press at this date, but the 1930 exhibition was highly praised in *The Times*.

Norah Braden remained with Katharine Pleydell-Bouverie until 1936 and was associated with the glaze experimentation which was an important feature of the Coleshill pottery at this time. She then went to teach at the Brighton College of Art, and after the war also at Camberwell and Chichester, where she still lives.

Norah Braden ceased potting in the early 1950s and so examples of her work are very rare.

**157 Deep bowl on high foot** Diameter 16 cm (6¼ in), height 13.5 cm (5¼ in)
Ash glaze on pale leaf-sprig patterning and bands in grey. Heavily crackled. Deeply
turned foot. Stoneware. Made *c*. 1925.
*Bought at The New Craftsman, St Ives in 1984. Previously in the collection of Bernard Leach.*

# William Marshall

William Marshall was born in St Ives in 1923, and went to work at the Leach Pottery in 1938. After the war he worked at the pottery continuously until 1977, his work reflecting both the English and Oriental influences which pervaded the pottery over four decades. Towards the end of his period at St Ives many of the larger individual pots designed and later decorated by Bernard Leach were thrown by William Marshall, an example of a very successful creative partnership.

In 1977 he set up his own pottery at Lelant, near St Ives, building with his son Andrew a two-chambered wood- and oil-fired kiln.

Although he has drawn inspiration from many cultures, he states that it is his native Cornish landscape, with its lichen and moss-covered granite moors and the decorated Celtic crosses, which has influenced the shapes, glazes and textures of his varied work.

**158 Cane-handled teapot** Diameter (bowl) 18 cm (7 in), height (less handle) 12.5 cm (5 in) Glazed over dark slip with wax-resist pattern brush-painted on both sides. Lower section unglazed. Stoneware. WM inscribed and St Ives seal near unglazed foot. Made *c.* 1972.
*Date of acquisition unknown.*

**159 Pot** Diameter 21.5 cm (8½ in), height 22 cm (8¾ in)
Four lugs. Kaki glaze overall with white on top. Unturned base. Stoneware. WM and
St Ives seals obscured by glaze on side.
*Bought at the Leach Pottery, St Ives in 1971.*

**160 Cut-sided yunomi** Width 7.5 cm (2¾ in), height 9 cm (3½ in)
Porcelain. WM and small St Ives seals inside turned glazed foot. Made *c.* 1961.
*Date of acquisition unknown.*

**161 Yunomi** Width 8 cm (3¼ in), height 9.5 cm (3¾ in)
Brown kaki glaze outside with black on rim, green ash glaze inside. Stoneware. WM and St Ives seals inside glazed foot. Made *c.* 1961.
*Date of acquisition unknown.*

**162 Yunomi** Diameter 7.5 cm (3 in), height 8.5 cm (3¾ in)
Hakeme slip with grey glaze over. Brown spotting from iron in the clay. Stoneware. WM
and St Ives seals inside turned foot, under glaze.
*Bought at the Leach Pottery, St Ives in 1961.*

**163-68 Group of small yunomis**

**163** Diameter 6 cm (2½ in), height 5.5 cm (2¼ in). Tenmoku glaze overall with kaki dripped pattern. Stoneware. **164** Diameter 7 cm (2¾ in), height 5 cm (2 in). Brown glaze outside turned blue-grey by pale glaze overall. Stoneware. WM and small St Ives seals inside foot. **165** Diameter 7 cm (2¾ in), height 5.5 cm (2¼ in). Stamped star patterns on outside. Light glaze overall overlies darker glaze on outside. Stoneware. St Ives seal and 'England' on glazed turned foot. **166** Diameter 6 cm (2½ in), height 5.5 cm (2¼ in). Impressed repeating pattern filled with white slip, glazed overall with grey-green glaze Stoneware. **167** Diameter 7.5 cm (3 in), height 5.5 cm (2¼ in). White glaze inside and on upper part of outside overlapping with tenmoku on lower half. Stoneware. 'England' on foot and WM seal outside glazed foot. **168** Diameter 7 cm (2¾ in), height 5.5 cm (2¼ in). Tenmoku glaze overall. Stoneware.

*All bought at the Sybil Hansen Gallery, Kensington Church Walk, where they were used to serve drinks at the opening of an exhibition in 1973.*

**169 Jar** Width 16 cm (6¼ in), height 26 cm (10¼ in)
Raw glazed, with thin ash glaze on shoulder and inside. Stoneware. WM and small St Ives
seals, near unturned base.
*Bought at the Leach Pottery, St Ives in 1973.*

**170 Bowl** Diameter 28 cm (11 in), height 6.5 cm (2½ in)
Tenmoku glaze, with kaki painting inside and white glaze running over rim. Stoneware.
WM and St Ives seals near unturned base.
*Bought at the Penwith Gallery, Cornwall, in 1967.*

**171 Teapot** Diameter (bowl) 18.5 cm (7¼ in), height overall 15 cm (6 in)
Glazed in speckled greenish ash glaze over ladle splashes of white slip on both sides.
Stoneware.
*Bought at the Penwith Gallery, Cornwall in 1959.*

**172 Bowl on stem** Diameter 22.5 cm (8¾ in), height 12.5 cm (5 in)
Thrown in two pieces, jigger patterning on outside of rim. Pale-green glaze. Porcelain.
Two WM and small St Ives seals inside glazed hollow stem.
*Bought at the Leach Pottery at St Ives.*

# *The Leach School*

Young potters who trained at the Leach Pottery in St Ives are too numerous to mention individually. Over five decades, many were employed to make the standard range of domestic ware, and most produced work in the Leach/St Ives tradition. Several became distinguished potters in their own right, leaving to found potteries elsewhere. Longevity seems to be a characteristic of the Leach circle, but one potter who died tragically young was Kenneth Quick, whose work is represented here by pot No. 174, and possibly also No. 173. Shoji Hamada's third son Atsuya worked in the pottery in the 1950s, and his work is represented by pots 176 and 177.

**173 Open bowl** Diameter 15.5 cm (6 in), height 7.5 cm (3 in)
White slip painted under grey glaze gives spiral pattern near centre. Severe crawling on
outside. Stoneware. St Ives and individual (not decipherable) seals under glaze near
unglazed turned foot. Made in the 1950s.
*Bought at the Leach Pottery, St Ives in 1958.*

**174 Yunomi** Diameter 7.5 cm (3 in), height 9 cm (3½ in)
Pale grey glaze thick on outside from several
dippings. Brush-painted design in Hamada style in
liquid amber glaze on two sides. Stoneware. St Ives
and Kenneth Quick seals.
*Bought at the Leach Pottery, St Ives in 1958.*

**175 Yunomi** Diameter 8 cm (3 in), height 9 cm (3½ in)
Horizontal ribbed design largely obscured by
tenmoku glaze outside, kaki glaze inside. Stoneware.
St Ives and (?)TC seals inside turned and glazed foot.
Made in 1958.
*Date of acquisition unknown.*

**176 Yunomi** Diameter 8.5 cm (3½ in), height 9.5 cm (3¾ in)
Impressed pattern. Tenmoku glaze inside and
overlapping with grey felspathic glaze. Stoneware.
St Ives seal inside foot and 'England' on side of foot.
Probably made by Atsuya Hamada, *c.* 1958.
*Date of acquisition unknown.*

**177 Yunomi** Diameter 8.5 cm (3½ in), height 10 cm (4 in)
Horizontal ribbing and vertical slash pattern covered with
kaki glaze outside with crackled ash glaze inside and
running over rim. Stoneware. St Ives seal and 'England' on
foot. Probably made by Atsuya Hamada, *c.* 1958.
*Date of acquisition unknown.*

# Richard Batterham

Richard Batterham was born in 1936 and was first taught to throw by Don Potter at Bryanston School. He went to St Ives as a trainee at the Leach Pottery in 1957 and 1958. During his time in St Ives and in subsequent years he came to know or to meet all the potters whose work is included in this book.

Returning to Dorset in 1959, he built himself an oil fired two-chambered climbing kiln at Durweston in Dorset, alongside the house where he still lives. His intention was to make pots which would enrich rather than adorn life, and within a few years he had developed a range of pots to satisfy the needs of both the kitchen and the table. For over a quarter of a century he has worked alone, firing the kiln five or six times a year. Richard Batterham has long been regarded as a unique domestic pottery maker working within the Leach tradition, although his distinctive pots are instantly recognizable as his own. He has exhibited in London since 1964, most recently at the Victoria and Albert Museum's Crafts Shop in 1990, and exhibitions of his work have also been held in Oxford, Blandford, Heidelberg, Hamburg, Rotterdam and Stockholm.

LEFT **178 Small teapot** Width (bowl) 11.5 cm (4½ in), height overall 11 cm (4¼ in)
Sides indented. Pulled handle. Poplar ash glaze mottled with iron from clay. Stoneware.
*Bought at the Durweston Pottery in 1980.*

CENTRE **179 Teapot** Width (bowl) 14 cm (5½ in), height overall 14 cm (5½ in)
Ten cut sides. Pulled handle. Salt glazed over slip and over bare clay on rim of lid.
Stoneware.
*Bought at the Durweston Pottery in 1987.*

RIGHT **180 Small teapot** Width (bowl) 10 cm (4 in), height overall 11 cm (4¼ in)
Cut sides, concave base. Salt glaze over all of outside. Stoneware.
*Bought at the Crafts Centre of Great Britain in 1984.*

**182 Lidded mustard pot**
Width 8 cm (3¼ in), height overall 7 cm
(2¾ in)
Green glaze inside, salt glaze outside.
Stoneware.
*Bought at the Durweston Pottery in 1984.*

**183 Lidded pot**
Width 9 cm (3½ in), height overall 7.5 cm (3 in)
Squared off from outside and inside and
diagonal patterning on faces. Dark-green
glaze inside and outside, salt glaze
outside. Stoneware.
*Bought at the Durweston Pottery in 1980.*

**184 Lidded pot**
Width 8.5 cm (3½ in), height overall 8 cm
(3¼ in)
Green glaze inside. Salt glaze outside.
Stoneware.
*Bought in 1980.*

**185 Large lidded jar** Width 18 cm (7 in), height overall 23 cm (9 in)
Added band on lid. Ash glaze on lid and running into iron glaze on pot. Stoneware.
*Date of acquisition unknown.*

**186 Teapot** Width (bowl) 12.5 cm (5 in), height overall 13 cm (5¼ in)
Pulled handle. Chatter-tooling on shoulder. Salt glazed. Green glaze inside. Stoneware.
*Bought at the Durweston Pottery in 1980.*

**187 Bowl** Diameter 21 cm (8¼ in), height 10.5 cm (4 in)
Rills outside, incised rings inside. Crackled oak ash glaze inside, and iron glaze on ochre
slip outside. Slip inside turned foot. Stoneware.
*Bought at the Durweston Pottery in 1980.*

**188 Lidded jar**
Width 11 cm (4¼ in), height overall 13 cm
(5 in)
Poplar ash glaze. Stoneware.
*Bought at the Durweston Pottery in 1987.*

**189 Lidded jar**
Width 14 cm (5½ in), height overall 17 cm (6¾ in)
Rilled on cylindrical sides, star pattern
cut into lid. Ash glaze. Stoneware.
*Bought at the Crafts Centre of Great Britain
in 1984.*

**190 Lidded jar**
Width 12 cm (4¾ in), height overall 13 cm
(5¼ in)
Star pattern cut into lid with iron glaze,
wiped near base. Stoneware.
*Bought at the Durweston Pottery in 1984.*

**191 Lidded jar** Width 13.5 cm (5½ in), height overall 15 cm (5¾ in)
Ribbed from inside to make squarish form. Tooled at neck and with turning on top of lid
to make spiral decoration. Glazed inside and outside with poplar ash glaze. Stoneware.
Made in 1983.
*Bought at the Durweston Pottery in 1983.*

**192 Lidded jar** Width 10 cm (4 in), height overall
14.5 cm (5¾ in)
Unglazed near rim. Banding emphasised by glaze.
Stoneware.
*Bought at the Durweston Pottery in 1987.*

**193 Lidded jar** Width 10 cm (4 in), height overall
14.5 cm (5¾ in)
Unglazed near rim. Banded and cut decoration. Dark
glaze inside and outside.   Stoneware.
*Bought at the Durweston Pottery in 1987.*

185

**194 Small vase** Width 6.5 cm (2½ in), height 7.5 cm (3 in)
Squared off from outside and inside. Incised bands and salt glaze. Mottled grey and light
brown. Stoneware.
*Bought in 1980.*

**195 Covered box** Diameter 9 cm (3½ in), height overall 5.5 cm (2¼ in)
Star pattern cut into lid. Glazed dark honey-brown inside and outside. Stoneware.
*Bought at the Durweston Pottery in 1987.*

**196 Small vase** Width 6.5 cm (2½ in), height 7.5 cm (3 in)
Squared off. Incised bands. Salt glaze over slip, dark grey and brown mottling. Stoneware.
*Bought in 1980.*

**197, 198, 199 Three bowls** Diameter (all) 13.5 cm (4¼ in), height (all) 5.5 cm (2¼ in)
Tableware bowls with incised and chatter-tooling inside and outside, distinguished by a
particularly beautiful glaze. Turned unglazed feet. Stoneware. Made *c*. 1980.
*Date of acquisition unknown.*

**200 Lidded jar** Width 20 cm (8 in), height overall 21.5 cm (8½ in)
Squared off from outside and inside. Chatter-tooling on banded shoulder. Star pattern cut
into lid. Oak ash inside. Green ash glaze on lid and shoulder, dark-olive glaze on body of
pot. Stoneware. Made in 1987.
*Bought at the Durweston Pottery in 1987.*

**201 Dish** Diameter 15.5 cm (6 in), height 4.5 cm (1¾ in)
Incised ring and cross combing. Pooled and crazed ash glaze, runny on the outside.
Stoneware.
*Date of acquisition unknown.*

**202 Dish**
Diameter 19.5 cm (7¾ in), height 4.5 cm
(1¾ in)
Pale-green glaze on inside, thickening to
emphasise the raised ring. Porcelain.
*Bought at the Durweston Pottery in 1983.*

**203 Bowl**
Diameter 16.5 cm (6½ in), height 7.5 cm (3 in)
Chatter patterning inside lower internal
ring. Ash glaze. Glazed inside turned
foot. Porcelain.
*Bought at the Durweston Pottery in 1983.*

**204 Bowl**
Diameter 11 cm (4¼ in), height 5 cm
(1¾ in)
Two incised rings inside. Pale ash glaze.
Glazed inside turned foot. Porcelain.
*A gift from the potter, 1983.*

**205 Porcelain bowl** Diameter 17.5 cm (7 in), height 7 cm (2¾ in)
Raised ring inside, emphasised by thickening of the glaze. Repeating pattern on outside
only. White porcelain glaze. Glazed inside turned footring.
*A gift from the potter, 1984.*

# Selected bibliography

Arts Council of Great Britain *Bernard Leach - 50 years a Potter* (catalogue) London 1961
Cardew, Michael *Pioneer Pottery* London 1969
    ... *A Pioneer Potter* London 1988
Crafts Council *Katharine Pleydell-Bouverie, a Potter's Life 1895-1985* London 1986
Hamada, Shoji *Pottery by Shoji Hamada* Tokyo 1935
Honey, William B. *Art of the Potter* London 1946
Leach, Bernard *A Potter's Book* London 1940, 1989
    ... *A Potter's Portfolio* London 1951
    ... *A Potter in Jap    -1954* London 1960
    ... *A Potter's Wo.    ondon* 1967
    ... *Har   'a Potter* Tokyo, New York 1975
    ... *A .   r's Challenge* London 1976
    ... *Beyond East and West* London 1978
Peterson, Susan *Shoji Hamada, A Potter's Way and Work* New York 1974, 1981, 1984
Pleydell-Bouverie, Katharine, et al *A Chance Account* (catalogue) Crafts Study Centre, Bath 1980
Rose, Muriel *Artist Potters in England* 1955, 1970 (revised)
Victoria and Albert Museum *The Art of Bernard Leach* (catalogue) London 1977
Wakefield, Hugh 'The Leach Tradition' in *Crafts* No 6, 1974
Wingfield Digby, George *The Work of the Modern Potter in England* London 1952
Yanagi, Soetsu *Bernard Leach* Tokyo 1966

# Acknowledgements

The authors would like to acknowledge the help given in the
preparation of this book by Richard Batterham, Janet Leach,
Philip Lindley and, in particular, Belinda Wingfield Digby,
for her assistance at all stages of its production.